Cambridge **Discovery Education**™

▶ **INTERACTIV**

Series editor: B

G000128091

SPORT, GAME, OR HOBBY?

A2⁺

Simon Beaver

CAMBRIDGE
UNIVERSITY PRESS

DISCOVERY
EDUCATION™

CAMBRIDGE UNIVERSITY PRESS
Cambridge, New York, Melbourne, Madrid, Cape Town,
Singapore, São Paulo, Delhi, Mexico City

Cambridge University Press
32 Avenue of the Americas, New York, NY 10013-2473, USA

www.cambridge.org
Information on this title: www.cambridge.org/9781107686588

First published 2014

Printed in Hong Kong, China, by Golden Cup Printing Company Limited

A catalog record for this publication is available from the British Library.

Library of Congress Cataloging-in-Publication Data

Beaver, Simon.
  Sport, game, or hobby? / Simon Beaver.
    pages cm. -- (Cambridge discovery interactive readers)
  ISBN 978-1-107-68658-8 (pbk. : alk. paper)
  1. Sports--Juvenile literature. 2. English language--Textbooks for foreign speakers. 3. Readers
(Elementary) I. Title.

GV705.4.B43 2013
796--dc23

                            2013021203

ISBN 978-1-107-68658-8

Additional resources for this publication at www.cambridge.org

Cambridge University Press has no responsibility for the persistence or
accuracy of URLs for external or third-party Internet Web sites referred to in
this publication and does not guarantee that any content on such Web sites is,
or will remain, accurate or appropriate.

Layout services, art direction, book design, and photo research: Q2ABillSMITH GROUP
Editorial services: Hyphen S.A.
Audio production: CityVox, New York
Video production: Q2ABillSMITH GROUP

Contents

Before You Read: Get Ready! 4

CHAPTER 1
When Is a Sport Not a Sport?.................. 6

CHAPTER 2
Machine Sports.................................... 10

CHAPTER 3
Electronic Competition............................ 14

CHAPTER 4
Discipline Sports 18

CHAPTER 5
Animal Sports...................................... 22

CHAPTER 6
What Do You Think? 24

After You Read.................................... 26

Answer Key 28

Glossary

Before You Read: Get Ready!

What's the difference between a game and a sport? Sometimes, it's not easy to decide.

Words to Know

Look at the pictures. Complete the sentences with the correct words.

athletes   fan   fight   judge   shooting

1. I love baseball! I'm a big _____.
2. He's terrible at _____. He can't hit anything.
3. The _____ said she was the winner.
4. You can see the best _____ in the world at the Olympics.
5. Don't _____, children! There's enough candy for both of you!

Words to Know

Read the paragraph. Then complete the sentences with the correct highlighted words.

Do you practice a sport? I enjoy a lot of activities, like walking, reading, and playing video games, but I love basketball the most. It's not a hi-tech sport – no machines or science needed. You just have to learn the rules – what you can and can't do – and some skills, like how to make the ball do what you want. They say the important thing in a game is to take part and do your best. But what I want most is for us to get more points than the other team.

1. You need special _____ for that job: computers, languages, and math.

2. I have a _____ refrigerator – it tells me when I need to buy things!

3. We played a game in class today. Sarah got the most _____ and won.

4. They have many _____ for children at the science museum. They can build things and play games.

5. If you want to be a good dancer, you should _____ every day.

6. You can't eat in the library – it's against the _____ .

7. You should _____ in the conversation and say what you think.

CHAPTER 1

When Is a Sport Not a Sport?

WHAT EXACTLY IS A SPORT? PEOPLE OFTEN BELIEVE THEY KNOW – UNTIL YOU ASK THEM TO EXPLAIN.

When we hear the word "sport," we usually think of football, basketball, the Olympic Games, and things like that.

But isn't a sport more than that? Different people have different answers.

Some people think that an activity must have a winner to be a sport. But does that mean that running and swimming are only sports when you are in a race or competition? What about when you try to improve your own running or swimming? Aren't you trying to win against yourself? Is that a sport?

ANALYZE

What's your favorite sport? What special skills do people need for this sport?

Many people think that a sport must be hard for your body. But what about if you only need to think? Look at chess. There are chess competitions and chess stars. So is chess a sport?

And do you need to be strong and fit to take part in a sport? What about Olympic shooting? You don't have to be strong to do that.

One thing all sports need is **skill**. A skill is something special you can do better than others. It's often a thing you learn, but some people have natural skills. Most people can learn to play football. But to be a really good football player, you need to be naturally quick and move well.

Then there are hobbies. Hobbies are special activities that we like to spend our time doing when we aren't working. So a sport can be a hobby, but not all hobbies are sports. Painting and cooking are hobbies. But no one calls those things sports.

If your hobby is looking after your garden, people don't call it a sport. But if you climb mountains – if you're a mountaineer – many people will say you're taking part in a sport. Maybe that's because mountaineers compete – in other words, they try to do better than other climbers.

But gardeners compete, too! Maybe you have flower shows in your town with prizes for the best flowers. So why don't we call that a sport?

Finally, what are games? Football is a game – but chess, video games, and **hide** and seek[1] are games, too, each with its own rules.

Is a game something we do just for fun? That's also true for hobbies. And some games are clearly sports, but people don't agree about others.

This book looks at different activities. Some are watched by crowds. For some, you have to be fit and strong; for others, you have to be smart or quick. But are they sports, games, or hobbies? You decide.

[1]**hide and seek:** A game in which children go somewhere that's hard to find (they hide) and others look for (seek) them.

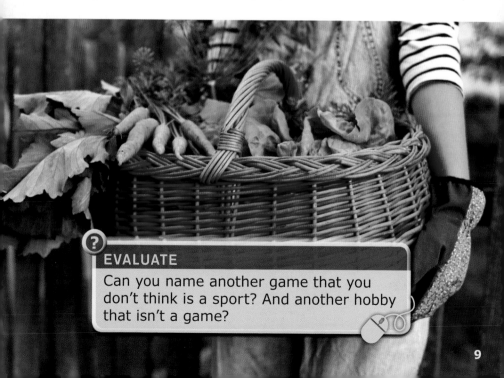

?
EVALUATE
Can you name another game that you don't think is a sport? And another hobby that isn't a game?

CHAPTER 2

Machine Sports

SOME PEOPLE SAY IT CAN'T BE A SPORT IF YOU USE A MACHINE. BUT NOT EVERYONE AGREES.

Some sports use hi-tech machines. They can be as important as the people who use them – or even more important.

How about car racing? Fans know that a driver can be the greatest in the world one year and do badly the next. Why? Maybe because another driver has a better car that year. So is car racing a sport, or is it more a competition for car makers?

Probably both. Racing drivers must be strong, fit athletes. Car racing is very tiring. Formula 1 drivers lose as much as three kilograms of water from their body in just one race!

Racing drivers need to understand their car and the track or road they race on. They must think and do things very fast. And crowds watch. So we can say that car racing is a sport, but one for people and machines working together.

What about flying? Today, it's more like a job or a hobby. But a century ago, people like Louis Blériot and Amelia Earhart were stars. They were the first to fly across seas and oceans at a time when it was very dangerous. Some of them died! So why did they do it? To be first. To be better than everyone else. Isn't that what sports is all about?

Video Quest

Smashing Pumpkins!

Watch this video about people who smash, or break, pumpkins as a hobby. How do they smash them?

How about a game played since 2000 called geocaching? Is it a sport?

In geocaching, people use their GPS or smartphone to find a hidden box, or cache.

Before geocaching, people played the same kind of game. They had to find a written note that sent them somewhere to find another note and finally get to the cache.

Geocachers use the Internet to tell other people where to find caches. They often hide boxes in places that are very hard to get to: on a mountain or along a river. There are caches in cities, too, and even one on the International Space Station!

Inside the caches there are lists where finders can add their names. There are also prizes that aren't too expensive, like unusual money or small toys. There could also be "travel bugs" with numbers on them. Geocachers move these travel bugs from cache to cache. They put the numbers from the travel bug on the Internet. Then other geocachers can follow online where the travel bugs go.

If finders take prizes from a cache, the rule is that they must leave other prizes that cost the same, so the box is always full.

Many players say that geocaching is a sport. Other people say it isn't. But if enough people think something is a sport, isn't it? Even if it uses hi-tech machines?

? ANALYZE
Which sports don't use machines? Are hi-tech running shoes "machines," too?

CHAPTER 3

Electronic Competition

TODAY, ELECTRONIC COMPETITION IS POPULAR: BUT IS VIDEO GAMING A SPORT?

Most young people now play video games. Thirty years ago, they were very simple games on small screens in big machines. Now, we can play video games on computers, TVs, or phones. The pictures look almost real, with amazing art, colors, and sounds.

Before, only one or two people could play. Then at-home consoles[2] arrived in the 1980s. Several people could play together. There were racing games, different sports like football or tennis, and quests. Quest players had a **goal** – maybe to help a queen in danger. They traveled through strange places and did many difficult things to win.

[2]**console:** a box used to play video games on a TV

In the 2000s, more and more people got computers and the Internet. Now, many people around the world can play the same game together. There are three main kinds:

- shooter games, with a lot of fighting

- strategy games, where players have to think and plan

- role-playing games, where players become one of the stars of the story

Today, there are video game competitions in stadiums. Many people come to play, and crowds come to watch. The best players are very skilled and fast. Like athletes!

So, video games have now joined football and baseball as stadium sports.

In Chapter 2, we asked if something is really a sport if people use hi-tech help. What about robot sport, where robots do things *instead of* people?

Every year in California, there's a big meeting called RoboGames. It's the world's biggest robot competition open to everyone. There are over 50 different kinds of competitions for the robots. They include fighting robots that shoot out fire and hit other robots, walking humanoid[3] robots, and others that play sports.

Most of the games are for autonomous robots. Autonomous means that nobody **controls** them during the games. They "decide" what to do alone.

....

[3]**humanoid:** looks like a person

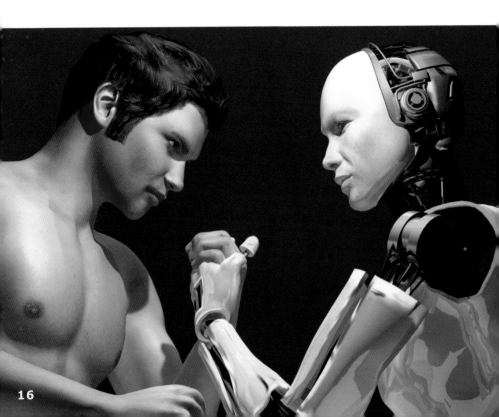

The people who started RoboGames wanted robot builders with different skills to meet and share ideas. The idea is that the games will help to improve the science of robotics.

Quite soon, we may see even more fantastic robot competitions. The Japanese company Honda has built a robot called ASIMO that can run! Running is easy for most people, but amazingly difficult for a humanoid robot. Robots like ASIMO could race against people one day!

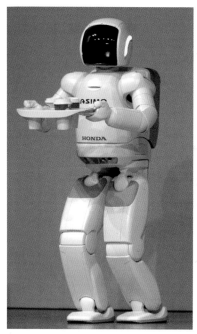

So what will tomorrow bring? In the 1970s we didn't have the smartphones, video games, and robots that we have today. What will we have in the 2020s and how will it change the world of hi-tech sports?

Asimo the robot

Video Quest

Robot Wars

Watch the video to learn about an amazing family. What has changed about the competition they are in?

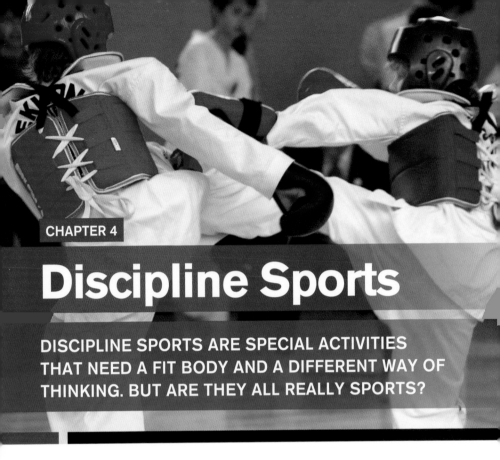

CHAPTER 4

Discipline Sports

DISCIPLINE SPORTS ARE SPECIAL ACTIVITIES THAT NEED A FIT BODY AND A DIFFERENT WAY OF THINKING. BUT ARE THEY ALL REALLY SPORTS?

Discipline means two things. First, a discipline is something you study. Second, if you "have discipline," it means you can do difficult or unpleasant things to reach a goal. In discipline sports, you work to improve your body, control your body, and also change the way you think.

Martial arts are popular everywhere in the world. A long time ago, people used them to fight in wars.[4] But today, martial arts, like karate and judo, are sports. To practice them, you must learn to be strong in both your body and your mind.[5]

[4]**war:** when two or more countries fight, it is a war
[5]**mind:** what you use to think

People who practice martial arts don't want to hurt or control others. The goal is just to improve yourself. People can do that alone – but they also enjoy competition!

Crowds watch taekwondo competitions. They're a part of the Olympic Games. So most people say they're sports.

But what about a martial art called tai chi? It's almost like dancing. You have to move your arms, body, and legs in special ways, often very slowly. In today's competitions, people don't fight. The competitions are like a show, with judges to choose the winners. So is tai chi a sport? Or is it more like a beauty competition?

Competition yoga is perhaps even harder to understand. Many people who practice yoga meditate. That means they try to **relax** and forget the world around them. To help them do this, they hold their bodies in special **positions**.

Yoga was started by people in India who believed that after we die, we're born again in another body. Today, people who believe this say that practicing yoga and meditation help a person to forget the world and all the usual things that people want. Then they can be a better person in their future lives.

But if yoga is about improving yourself and forgetting the world around you, why have competitions? That isn't really the idea of yoga, is it?

Rajashree Choudhury was born in India. She's the head of USA Yoga. She wants yoga to be in the Olympics. She says that competition yoga isn't about meditation, it's a sport.

Roseanne Harvey from Canada doesn't agree. She has practiced yoga for 15 years and writes about it on the Internet. She says yoga means not getting angry, not hurting other people, and understanding them and yourself. She says most yoga classes tell people *not* to compete. She also thinks that if people see competitions, they may not want to practice yoga because it looks so hard.

So are all of these disciplines sports? Or just some of them? Different people have different ideas.

CHAPTER 5

Animal Sports

PEOPLE USE ANIMALS IN COMPETITIONS, BUT ARE THOSE COMPETITIONS SPORTS?

People have raced horses for centuries. Today, horse racing is one of the most popular sports in the world. In many countries, there are racetracks – stadiums where horses race. Owners pay a lot of money for the best horses and riders. Crowds go to see the races.

But what about other animal activities? Dog and cat shows are very popular. People make their animals look beautiful and healthy. They teach dogs to stand and walk in special ways for the judges. But can we call this a sport? Many people come to watch and there are winners, so maybe we can.

And falconry? For thousands of years, falconers have taught falcons to fly away, catch other birds, and bring them back. They take part in competitions. Fans watch. So is it a sport or a hobby? What do you think?

Video Quest

Faster Than a Falcon?

Watch the video to learn about this amazingly fast bird. How fast can it fly? What does the man have in his hand and why?

What Do You Think?

A game from Britain is becoming very popular in other countries: snooker. Here are the main rules:

- there are two players

- there is a special table, which is very big – about 3.7 meters long and 1.8 meters wide

- there are 22 balls: one white, 15 red, and six more of different colors

- players use cues – long pieces of wood – to hit only the white ball, which must then hit a colored ball

- players get **points** for hitting a colored ball into one of the six pockets around the sides of the table

- players must "pocket" a red ball first, then they can choose a different color ball

- there is one point for red, and two to seven points for the other colors

There are big snooker competitions in different countries. Large prizes are given, and the best players become rich! Crowds watch. Games are shown on TV.

Snooker fans say it's a sport. Others don't agree, perhaps because great snooker players don't have to be fit, fast, or strong. So do you think snooker is a sport? Why or why not?

After You Read

Choose (A) (True) or (B) (False). If the book does not tell you, choose (C) (Doesn't say).

1 Racing drivers are very fit.

  (A) True
  (B) False
  (C) Doesn't say

2 Geocachers can't use smartphones.

  (A) True
  (B) False
  (C) Doesn't say

3 The first video game was sold in 1972.

  (A) True
  (B) False
  (C) Doesn't say

4 An autonomous robot works on its own.

  (A) True
  (B) False
  (C) Doesn't say

5 Yoga began in China.

  (A) True
  (B) False
  (C) Doesn't say

6 Snooker players must keep one foot on the floor.

  (A) True
  (B) False
  (C) Doesn't say

People and Sports

Write down the names of three famous people who practice a sport. What sport do they practice? Give a reason (a different one each time) why you could call it a sport.

Person	Sport	Why it is a sport
1.		
2.		
3.		

Complete the Text

Complete the paragraph with the correct words from the box.

athletes   fan   judges   take part

People who run, swim, or jump in the Olympics are called

1 _____ . If you love to watch their sport, you are a

2 _____ . When they **3** _____ in a competition,

4 _____ watch to check that they follow the rules.

Answer Key

Words to Know, page 4
1 fan **2** shooting **3** judge **4** athletes **5** fight

Words to Know, page 5
1 skills **2** hi-tech **3** points **4** activities **5** practice
6 rules **7** take part

Analyze, page 7
Answers will vary.

Evaluate, page 9
Possible answers: Monopoly is a game, but not a sport.
Reading is a hobby, but not a game.

Video Quest, page 11
They use machines to shoot them through the air.

Analyze, page 13
Answers will vary.

Video Quest, page 17
The robots have to do more things.

Video Quest, page 23
It can fly 320 kilometers an hour. The man has meat in his
hand so the falcon will follow him.

True or False?, page 26
1 A **2** B **3** C **4** A **5** B **6** C

People and Sports, page 27
Answers will vary.

Complete the Text, page 27
1 athletes **2** fan **3** take part **4** judges